The Beatitudes for Today

with other
selected scriptures

COMPILED AND ILLUSTRATED BY
ROYAL V. CARLEY

The C. R. Gibson Company, *Publishers*
Norwalk, Connecticut

Blessed are the poor in spirit: for theirs is the kingdom of heaven.

Hast thou not known? hast thou not heard, that the everlasting God, the Lord, the Creator of the ends of the earth, fainteth not, neither is weary? there is no searching of his understanding. He giveth power to the faint; and to them that have no might he increaseth strength. Even the youths shall faint and be weary, and the young men shall utterly fall: But they that wait upon the Lord shall renew their strength; they shall mount up with wings as eagles; they shall run, and not be weary; and they shall walk, and not faint.   *Isaiah 40:28-31.*

FOR STACY LYN

ACKNOWLEDGMENTS
Thanks are due to the following:
Linton Whittles for photograph on page 25;
Carl Moreus for photographs on page 18.

And he spake this parable unto certain which trusted in
themselves that they were righteous, and despised others:
Two men went up into the temple to pray; the one a
Pharisee, and the other a publican. The Pharisee stood and
prayed thus with himself, God, I thank thee, that I am
not as other men are, extortioners, unjust, adulterers, or
even as this publican. I fast twice in the week, I give tithes
of all that I possess. And the publican, standing afar off,
would not lift up so much as his eyes unto heaven, but
smote upon his breast, saying, God be merciful to me a
sinner. I tell you, this man went down to his house
justified rather than the other: for every one that exalteth
himself shall be abased; and he that humbleth himself
shall be exalted.   *Luke 18:9-14.*

Blessed are they that mourn: for they shall be comforted.

From the end of the earth will I cry unto thee, when my heart is overwhelmed: lead me to the rock that is higher than I.   *Psalm 61:2*

I will lift up mine eyes unto the hills, from whence cometh my help. My help cometh from the Lord, which made heaven and earth. He will not suffer thy foot to be moved: he that keepeth thee will not slumber. Behold, he that keepeth Israel shall neither slumber nor sleep.

Psalm 121:1-4.

Blessed be God, even the Father
of our Lord Jesus Christ, the
Father of mercies, and the God of
all comfort; Who comforteth us
in all our tribulation, that we may
be able to comfort them which
are in any trouble, by the comfort
wherewith we ourselves are
comforted of God.
II Corinthians 1:3,4.

Now our Lord Jesus Christ
himself, and God, even our Father,
which hath loved us, and hath
given us everlasting consolation
and good hope through grace,
Comfort your hearts, and stablish
you in every good word and work.
II Thessalonians 2:16,17.

In the multitude of my thoughts
within me thy comforts delight
my soul. *Psalm 94:19.*

Although the fig tree shall not
blossom, neither shall fruit be in
the vines; the labour of the olive
shall fail, and the fields shall yield
no meat; the flock shall be cut off
from the fold, and there shall be
no herd in the stalls: Yet I will
rejoice in the Lord, I will joy in the
God of my salvation.
Habakkuk 3:17,18.

Blessed are the meek: for they shall inherit the earth.

Come unto me, all ye that labour and are heavy laden, and I will give you rest. Take my yoke upon you, and learn of me; for I am meek and lowly in heart: and ye shall find rest unto your souls. *Matthew 11:28,29.*

For ye see your calling, brethren, how that not many wise men after the flesh, not many mighty, not many noble, are called: But God hath chosen the foolish things of the world to confound the wise; and God hath chosen the weak things of the world to confound the things which are mighty; And base things of the world, and things which are despised, hath God chosen, yea, and things which are not, to bring to nought things that are. *I Corinthians 1:26-28.*

I therefore, the prisoner of the Lord, beseech you that ye walk worthy of the vocation wherewith ye are called. With all lowliness and meekness, with longsuffering, forbearing one another in love; Endeavouring to keep the unity of the Spirit in the bond of peace. *Ephesians 4:1-3.*

My sheep hear my voice, and I know them, and they follow me: And I give unto them eternal life; and they shall never perish, neither shall any man pluck them out of my hand.

John 10:27,28.

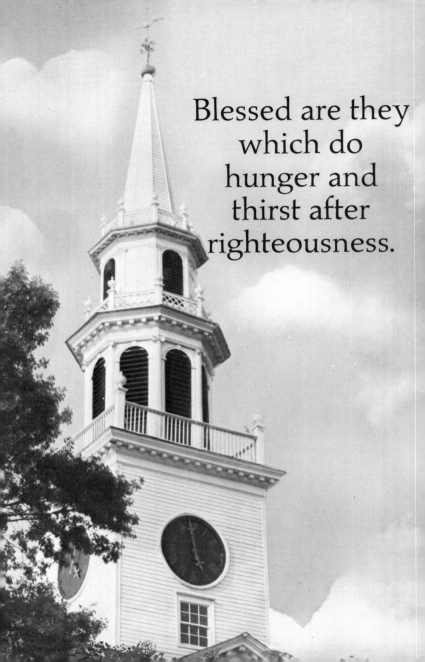

Blessed are they which do hunger and thirst after righteousness.

Blessed are the undefiled in the way, who walk in the law of the Lord. Blessed are they that keep his testimonies, and that seek him with the whole heart.   *Psalm 119:1,2.*

And be found in him, not having mine own righteousness, which is of the law, but that which is through the faith of Christ, the righteousness which is of God by faith.

Philippians 3:9.

For therein is the righteousness of God revealed from faith to faith: as it is written, The just shall live by faith.

Romans 1:17.

Wherefore seeing we also are compassed about with so great a cloud of witnesses, let us lay aside every weight, and the sin which doth so easily beset us, and let us run with patience the race that is set before us, Looking unto Jesus the author and finisher of our faith; who for the joy that was set before him endured the cross, despising the shame, and is set down at the right hand of the throne of God.   *Hebrews 12:1;2.*

The Lord is my shepherd; I shall not want. He maketh me to lie down in green pastures: he leadeth me beside the still waters. He restoreth my soul: he leadeth me in the paths of righteousness for his name's sake.   *Psalm 23:1-3.*

for they shall be filled.

He layeth up sound wisdom for the righteous: he is a buckler to them that walk uprightly. *Proverbs 2:7.*

And the scripture was fulfilled which saith, Abraham believed God, and it was imputed unto him for righteousness: and he was called the Friend of God. *James 2:23.*

Blessed be the God and Father of our Lord Jesus Christ, who hath blessed us with all spiritual blessings in heavenly places in Christ. *Ephesians 1:3.*

But of him are ye in Christ Jesus, who of God is made unto us wisdom, and righteousness, and sanctification, and redemption. *I Corinthians 1:30.*

Even the righteousness of God which is by faith of Jesus Christ unto all and upon all them that believe: for there is no difference. *Romans 3:22.*

For I will pour water upon him that is thirsty, and floods upon the dry ground: I will pour my spirit upon thy seed, and my blessing upon thine offspring: and they shall spring up as among the grass, as willows by the water courses. *Isaiah 44:3,4.*

But seek ye first the kingdom of God, and his righteousness; and all these things shall be added unto you. *Matthew 6:33.*

Blessed are the merciful:

And Jesus answering said, A certain man went down from Jerusalem to Jericho, and fell among thieves, which stripped him of his raiment, and wounded him, and departed, leaving him half dead. And by chance there came down a certain priest that way: and when he saw him, he passed by on the other side. And likewise a Levite, when he was at the place, came and looked on him, and passed by on the other side. But a certain Samaritan, as he journeyed, came where he was: and when he saw him, he had compassion on him, And went to him, and bound up his wounds, pouring in oil and wine, and set him on his own beast, and brought him to an inn, and took care of him. And on the morrow when he departed, he took out two pence, and gave them to the host, and said unto him, Take care of him; and whatsoever thou spendest more, when I come again, I will repay thee. Which now of these three, thinkest thou, was neighbour unto him that fell among the thieves? And he said, He that shewed mercy on him. Then said Jesus unto him, Go, and do thou likewise.

Luke 10:30-37.

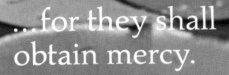

...for they shall obtain mercy.

Bless the Lord, O my soul: and all that is within me, bless his holy name. Bless the Lord, O my soul, and forget not all his benefits: Who forgiveth all thine iniquities; who healeth all thy diseases; Who redeemeth thy life from destruction; who crowneth thee with lovingkindness and tender mercies; Who satisfieth thy mouth with good things; so that thy youth is renewed like the eagle's. The Lord is merciful and gracious, slow to anger, and plenteous in mercy. He will not always chide: neither will he keep his anger for ever. He hath not dealt with us after our sins; nor rewarded us according to our iniquities. For as the heaven is high above the earth, so great is his mercy toward them that fear him. As far as the east is from the west, so far hath he removed our transgressions from us. Like as a father pitieth his children, so the Lord pitieth them that fear him. For he knoweth our frame; he remembereth that we are dust. *Psalm 103:1-5, 8-14.*

The Lord is gracious, and full of compassion; slow to anger, and of great mercy.   *Psalm 145:8.*

Thus speaketh the Lord of hosts, saying, Execute true judgment, and shew mercy and compassions every man to his brother.   *Zechariah 7:9.*

The Lord is my strength and my shield; my heart trusted in him, and I am helped: therefore my heart greatly rejoiceth; and with my song will I praise him.   *Psalm 28:7.*

I sought the Lord, and he heard me, and delivered me from all my fears.   *Psalm 34:4.*

I love the Lord, because he hath heard my voice and my supplications. Because he hath inclined his ear unto me, therefore will I call upon him as long as I live.   *Psalm 116:1,2.*

Blessed are the pure in heart: for they shall see God.

Who shall ascend into the hill of the Lord? or who shall stand in his holy place? He that hath clean hands, and a pure heart; who hath not lifted up his soul unto vanity, nor sworn deceitfully. He shall receive the blessing from the Lord, and righteousness from the God of his salvation.
Psalm 24:3-5.

Blessed is the man that walketh not in the counsel of the ungodly, nor standeth in the way of sinners, nor sitteth in the seat of the scornful. But his delight is in the law of the Lord; and in his law doth he meditate day and night. And he shall be like a tree planted by the rivers of water, that bringeth forth his fruit in his season; his leaf also shall not wither; and whatsoever he doeth shall prosper.
Psalm 1:1-3.

Let the words of my mouth, and the meditation of my heart, be acceptable in thy sight, O Lord, my strength, and my redeemer. *Psalm 19:14.*

Finally, brethren, whatsoever things are true, whatsoever things are honest, whatsoever things are just, whatsoever things are pure, whatsoever things are lovely, whatsoever things are of good report; if there be any virtue, and if there be any praise, think on these things.
Philippians 4:8.

Blessed are the peacemakers: for they shall be called the children of God.

. . . the wisdom that is from above is first pure, then peaceable, gentle, and easy to be intreated, full of mercy and good fruits, without partiality, and without hypocrisy. And the fruit of righteousness is sown in peace of them that make peace.   *James 3:17,18.*

Mark the perfect man, and behold the upright: for the end of that man is peace.   *Psalm 37:37.*

Follow peace with all men, and holiness, without which no man shall see the Lord.   *Hebrews 12:14.*

Let us therefore follow after the things which make for peace, and things wherewith one may edify another.
                                                     Romans 14:19.

Finally, brethren, farewell. Be perfect, be of good comfort, be of one mind, live in peace; and the God of love and peace shall be with you.   *II Corinthians 13:11.*

Blessed are they who are persecuted for righteousness' sake: for theirs is the kingdom of heaven.

Lord, how are they increased that trouble me! many are they that rise up against me. Many there be which say of my soul, There is no help for him in God. Selah. But thou, O Lord, art a shield for me; my glory, and the lifter up of mine head. I cried unto the Lord with my voice, and he heard me out of his holy hill. Selah. I laid me down and slept; I awaked; for the Lord sustained me. I will not be afraid of ten thousands of people, that have set themselves against me round about. Arise, O Lord; save me, O my God: for thou hast smitten all mine enemies upon the cheek bone; thou hast broken the teeth of the ungodly. Salvation belongeth unto the Lord: thy blessing is upon thy people. Selah.   *Psalm 3:1-8.*

No weapon that is formed against thee shall prosper; and every tongue that shall rise against thee in judgment thou shalt condemn. This is the heritage of the servants of the Lord, and their righteousness is of me, saith the Lord.
                                        Isaiah 54:17.

Blessed are ye, when men shall revile you, and persecute you, and shall say all manner of evil against you falsely, for my sake. Rejoice, and be exceedingly glad: for great is your reward in heaven: for so persecuted they the prophets which were before you.

Thrice was I beaten with rods, once was I stoned, thrice I suffered shipwreck, a night and a day I have been in the deep; In journeyings often, in perils of waters, in perils of robbers, in perils by mine own countrymen, in perils by the heathen, in perils in the city, in perils in the wilderness, in perils in the sea, in perils among false brethren.

II Corinthians 11:25,26.

Who shall separate us from the love of Christ? shall tribulation, or distress, or persecution, or famine, or nakedness, or peril, or sword? Nay, in all these things we are more than conquerors, through him that loved us.

Romans 8:35,37.

Yea, though I walk through the valley of the shadow of death, I will fear no evil: for thou art with me; thy rod and thy staff they comfort me.

Psalm 23:4.

And God shall wipe away all tears from their eyes; and there shall be no more death, neither sorrow, nor crying, neither shall there be any more pain: for the former things are passed away.

Revelation 21:4.

Therefore whosoever heareth these sayings of mine, and doeth them, I will liken him unto a wise man, which built his house upon a rock: And the rain descended, and the floods came, and the winds blew, and beat upon that house; and it fell not: for it was founded upon a rock. And every one that heareth these sayings of mine, and doeth them not, shall be likened unto a foolish man, which built his house upon the sand: And the rain descended, and the floods came, and the winds blew, and beat upon that house; and it fell: and great was the fall of it.

Matthew 7:24-27.

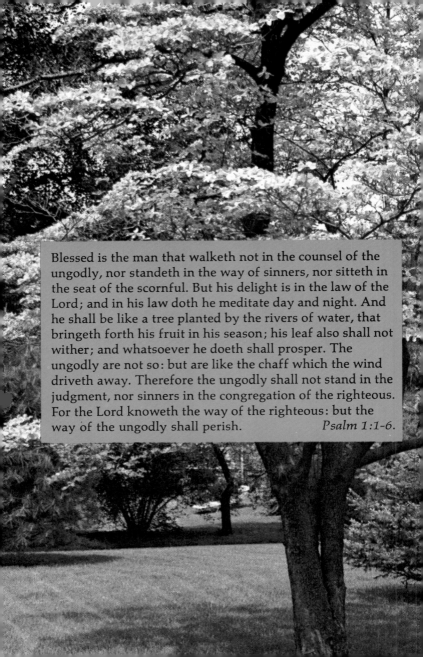

Blessed is the man that walketh not in the counsel of the ungodly, nor standeth in the way of sinners, nor sitteth in the seat of the scornful. But his delight is in the law of the Lord; and in his law doth he meditate day and night. And he shall be like a tree planted by the rivers of water, that bringeth forth his fruit in his season; his leaf also shall not wither; and whatsoever he doeth shall prosper. The ungodly are not so: but are like the chaff which the wind driveth away. Therefore the ungodly shall not stand in the judgment, nor sinners in the congregation of the righteous. For the Lord knoweth the way of the righteous: but the way of the ungodly shall perish. *Psalm 1:1-6.*